To: _____

From: _____

MW01014238

I LOVE YOU LIKE NO OTTER

Published by Sellers Publishing, Inc.

Copyright © 2018 Sellers Publishing, Inc.
Illustrations © 2018 Sophie Corrigan
All rights reserved.

Sellers Publishing, Inc.
161 John Roberts Road, South Portland, Maine 04106
Visit our Web site: www.sellerspublishing.com • E-mail: rsp@rsvp.com

Mary L. Baldwin, Managing Editor

Charlotte Cromwell, Production Editor

ISBN 13: 978-1-4162-4663-3

No portion of this book may be reproduced, stored in a
retrieval system, or transmitted in any form or by any means,
mechanical, electronic, photocopying, recording, or otherwise,
without the written permission of the publisher.

10 9 8 7 6 5 4 3 2 1

Printed in China.

I Love YOU LIKE NO OTTER

and other punny ways to say I love you

ILLUSTRATED BY SOPHiE CORRiGAN

SELLERS
PUBLISHING

I love spending
koality time with you.

You have my
seal of approval!

You're such a tweetheart.

I love
hanging out
with you.

I'm nuts about you.

I find you ribbiting.

You give me
porpoise.

I love you slow much!

Some bunny loves you!

I get
scenti-mental
when I think
about you.

I love you pig time!

You're
bamboo-tiful.

I love every-fin
about you!

Hedge-hug?

I whaley,
whaley love you.

I goat you babe.

Wanna go
on a picnic?
Alpaca lunch!

Waddle I do
until I see you?

I love you
and that's all rhino.

You
octopi
my heart.

Iguana be yours forever.

You're my
squeakheart.

I think you're
purrfectly great.

You're unbearably cute!

You're otter
this world.

You're my
wallabae.

I'll always stick by you!

I am bananas
for you.

You hold the kiwi
to my heart

You hold the kiwi
to my heart